United States Presidents

William McKinley

Paul Joseph
ABDO Publishing Company

visit us at
www.abdopub.com

Published by ABDO Publishing Company 4940 Viking Drive, Edina, Minnesota 55435.
Copyright © 2000 by Abdo Consulting Group, Inc. International copyrights reserved in all countries. No part of this book may be reproduced in any form without written permission from the publisher.

Printed in the United States.

Photo credits: Archive Photos, SuperStock, UPI/Corbis-Bettmann

Contributing editors: Robert Italia, Tamara L. Britton, K. M. Brielmaier, Kate A. Furlong

Library of Congress Cataloging-in-Publication Data

Joseph, Paul, 1970-
    William McKinley / Paul Joseph.
        p. cm. -- (United States presidents)
    Includes index.
    Summary: Discusses the personal life and military and political careers of the president who was assassinated in 1901 during his second term in office.
    ISBN 1-57765-244-4
1. McKinley, William, 1843-1901--Juvenile literature. 2. Presidents--United States--Biography--Juvenile literature. [1. McKinley, William, 1843-1901. 2. Presidents.] I. Title. II. Series: United States presidents (Edina, Minn.)
E711.6.J78   1999
973.8'8'092--dc21
    [B]
                                                            98-6608
                                                             CIP
                                                              AC

Contents

William McKinley

William McKinley was the twenty-fifth president of the United States. He served in the **Civil War**. He later worked as a teacher and a lawyer.

McKinley then got involved in politics. He was elected to the United States **House of Representatives**. Later, he was elected governor of Ohio.

In 1896, McKinley was elected president. He was easily elected to a second term in 1900. But only six months after his second term began, he was shot and killed.

Opposite page:
William McKinley

William McKinley (1843-1901)
Twenty-fifth President

BORN:	January 29, 1843
PLACE OF BIRTH:	Niles, Ohio
ANCESTRY:	Scots-Irish, English
FATHER:	William McKinley (1807-1892)
MOTHER:	Nancy Allison McKinley (1809-1897)
WIFE:	Ida Saxton (1847-1907)
CHILDREN:	Two girls
EDUCATION:	Poland Academy, Allegheny College
RELIGION:	Methodist
OCCUPATION:	Lawyer, teacher, clerk, soldier
MILITARY SERVICE:	Ohio 23rd Volunteers
POLITICAL PARTY:	Republican

OFFICES HELD: Member of U.S. House of Representatives, governor of Ohio

AGE AT INAUGURATION: 54

YEARS SERVED: 1897-1901

VICE PRESIDENT: Garret A. Hobart, 1897-1899
Theodore Roosevelt, 1901

DIED: September 14, 1901, New York, age 58

CAUSE OF DEATH: Assassination

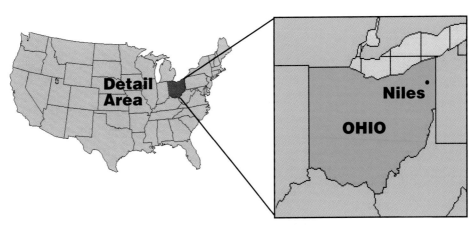

Birthplace of William McKinley

Young Will

William McKinley was born in Niles, Ohio, on January 29, 1843. He was the seventh of nine children born to William and Nancy McKinley. His father managed a **blast furnace** for **smelting** iron ore. His mother was active in the local Methodist church.

William was good at playing marbles. He was an excellent shot with his bow and arrows. And he liked to make and fly kites.

William's parents wanted their children to have a good education. In 1852, the family moved to Poland, Ohio, where there were better schools. In Poland, Will showed a great gift for public speaking. He became president of the debating society.

At 17, William graduated from high school. Then he attended Allegheny College in Meadville, Pennsylvania. But soon William got sick and had to go home to Ohio. For the next two years, he taught school in the Kerr school district, and worked part time as a clerk at the post office.

William McKinley's mother, Nancy

Civil War Hero

*I*n the 1850s, there were problems between the Northern and Southern states about slavery. The South wanted slavery and the North did not. The Southern states decided to leave the Union and start their own country.

In 1861, the **Civil War** began. McKinley enlisted as a **private** in the Ohio Volunteers. He served under future president Rutherford B. Hayes at the Battle of Antietam in 1862.

McKinley was in charge of making sure soldiers had proper meals and supplies. Because of his work in the war, McKinley was promoted to the rank of **lieutenant**. His courage and hard work continued throughout the Civil War. When the war ended, McKinley had the rank of **major**.

After the war, McKinley studied law in Poland, Ohio, at the law office of Charles Glidden. He also studied at the Albany Law School in Albany, New York. In 1867, he became a lawyer and moved to Canton, Ohio, where one of his sisters lived. He opened his first office in the new bank building. McKinley did well as a lawyer, and soon became an associate in Judge George W. Belden's law practice.

William McKinley as a lawyer

Politics and Family

*I*n 1869, McKinley was elected **prosecuting** attorney of Stark County, Ohio. He often defended and spoke out for unpopular causes, such as workers' rights. McKinley also defended the right of African Americans to vote.

While in Canton, McKinley met Ida Saxton. She was the daughter of a wealthy banker. Ida worked as a teller in her father's bank. In 1871, William and Ida were married.

On Christmas Day in 1871, the couple had a daughter they named Katie. On April 1, 1873, their daughter Ida was born.

After baby Ida's birth, several sad events occurred. In April of 1873, Mrs. McKinley's mother died. Five months later, baby Ida died. In June of 1876, Katie died. The McKinleys were filled with sorrow. McKinley continued in politics, but his wife was unhappy. She became sick and suffered from a nervous illness for the rest of her life.

In 1876, McKinley was elected to the United States **House of Representatives**. He served in the House for fourteen years.

Mrs. Ida McKinley

ngressman McKinley

cKinley was a hard working congressman. He introduced anti-liquor laws. He voted for the Pendleton Act of 1883 that required people to pass tests to get **civil service** jobs. He voted for the Chinese Exclusion Act that restricted Chinese **immigration** for ten years. He also voted for the Dependent Pension Bill that gave money to families of soldiers who fought in the **Civil War**.

McKinley served on the Committee on the Revision of the Laws. He also became chairman of the House Ways and Means Committee.

As chairman, McKinley helped write and pass the McKinley Tariff Act of 1890. This law put high taxes on **foreign** products that were sold in the United States.

McKinley thought this was good for the country. Businesses liked this new law. But most Americans did not like it. Good **foreign** products that people liked to buy were now too expensive.

McKinley thought the Tariff Act would improve the nation's economy in the long run. But Americans did not like having to pay more for foreign goods. In the election of 1890, McKinley was so unpopular that he lost.

Despite losing the election, McKinley was still considered a strong candidate for public office. The **Republicans** nominated him for governor of Ohio. McKinley easily won the election in 1891. He was re-elected in 1893. As governor, McKinley passed laws to tax railroads, telegraph and telephone operators, and foreign companies that did business in Ohio.

Republican leaders thought McKinley could be president. He decided to run for president in 1896.

The Making of the Twenty-fifth United States President

 **1843**

Born January 29 in Niles, Ohio

 **1852**

Family moves to Poland, Ohio

 **1860**

Graduates from high school; attends Allegheny College

 **1867**

Opens law office in Canton, Ohio

 **1869**

Elected prosecuting attorney

 **1871**

Marries Ida Saxton; daughter Katie is born

 **1890**

Passes McKinley Tariff Act; loses seat in House

1891

Elected governor of Ohio

 **1893**

Re-elected governor

William McKinley

"We want no war of conquest. . . . War should never be entered upon until every agency of peace has failed."

 **1861**

Civil War begins

 **1862**

Serves in Battle of Antietam

Historic Events
during McKinley's Presidency

Pierre and Marie Curie discover radium

Gold is discovered in the Klondike region of Yukon Territory, Canada

Tootsie Rolls first produced in New York by Leo Hirshfield

1873

Daughter Ida is born; she dies six months later

 **1876**

Daughter Katie dies; elected to U.S. House of Representatives

1896

Elected president

1898

Battleship USS *Maine* sinks; Spanish-American War begins

1900

Re-elected president

1901

Shot by assassin on September 6, dies September 14

PRESIDENTIAL YEARS

The Election of 1896

*I*n 1896, the **Republicans** nominated McKinley for president. Garret A. Hobart of New Jersey was nominated for vice president. The **Democrats** nominated William Jennings Bryan of Nebraska.

The biggest issue of the election was the money system. McKinley supported the gold standard. This meant that the nation's money represented gold. Because gold was rare, this meant that money would be worth more.

Bryan backed the free silver system. This meant that United States money represented both gold and silver. This would allow more money to be printed. But it would not be worth as much.

Bryan had the support of the poor and those in debt. To them, free silver meant more money available for people to use.

McKinley had the backing of the middle and upper class, bankers, and businessmen. Most of these people believed that the free silver system would hurt the economy.

McKinley easily won the election. He got almost 600,000 more popular votes than Bryan did.

William Jennings Bryan makes a campaign speech.

The Twenty-fifth President

*P*resident McKinley focused on **foreign** relations during his first term. The island of Cuba, 90 miles south of Florida, was owned by Spain. But the Cubans wanted freedom from Spain. There was a chance that a war would break out.

There were many Americans living in Cuba at this time. President McKinley was concerned for their safety. He sent the American battleship USS *Maine* to Cuba. On February 15, 1898, the *Maine* exploded and sank, killing 260 Americans.

Some people believed that Spain had blown up the ship. Some people thought the explosion was an accident. McKinley ordered an investigation by naval captains W. T. Sampson, F. E. Chadwick, and Lieutenant Commander William Potter. Their report said that the explosion was not an accident. Most people blamed Spain for the disaster.

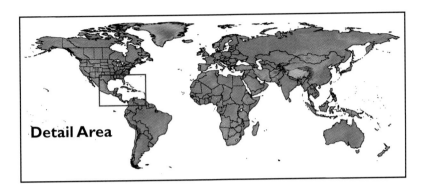

Detail Area

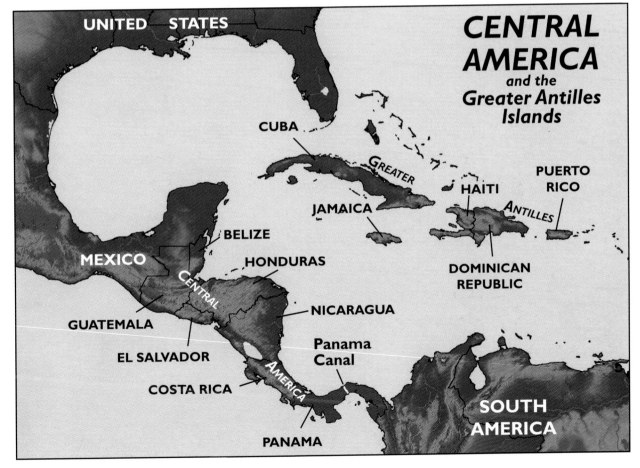

UNITED STATES

CENTRAL
AMERICA
and the
*Greater Antilles
Islands*

CUBA

GREATER

PUERTO
RICO

HAITI

ANTILLES

JAMAICA

BELIZE

MEXICO

HONDURAS

DOMINICAN
REPUBLIC

CENTRAL

NICARAGUA

GUATEMALA

Panama
Canal

EL SALVADOR

AMERICA

COSTA RICA

SOUTH
AMERICA

PANAMA

America declared war on Spain on April 25, 1898. The war ended quickly. The United States won. Spain and the United States signed a peace treaty in Paris on December 10, 1898.

The treaty freed Cuba from Spanish control and placed it under the United States' protection. The U.S. also acquired Puerto Rico, Guam, and the Philippines. The United States continued to claim territories. It took over the Hawaiian Islands and part of the Samoan Islands.

During his presidency, McKinley signed the Hay-Pauncefote Treaty. This treaty gave the United States **exclusive** ownership of the future Panama Canal. He signed the Dingley Tariff Act that allowed him to negotiate taxes for certain foreign goods.

McKinley also signed the Gold Standard Act that declared the gold dollar to be the standard of currency. And he sent troops to China to save Americans from the anti-foreigner uprising called the Boxer Rebellion.

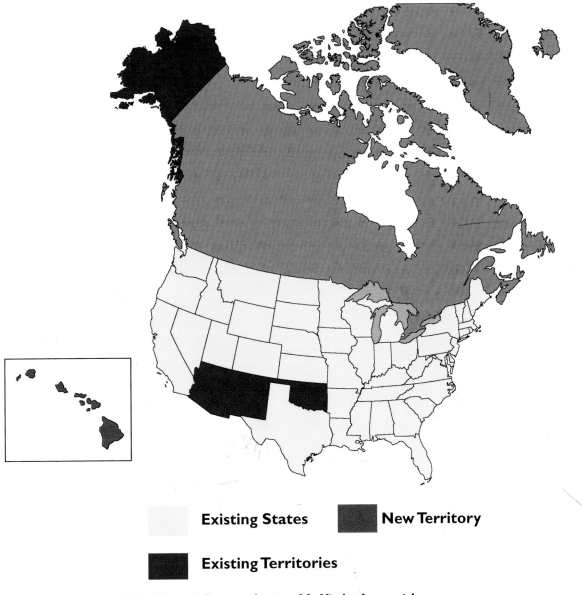

Existing States   New Territory

Existing Territories

The United States during McKinley's presidency

The Seven "Hats" of the U.S. President

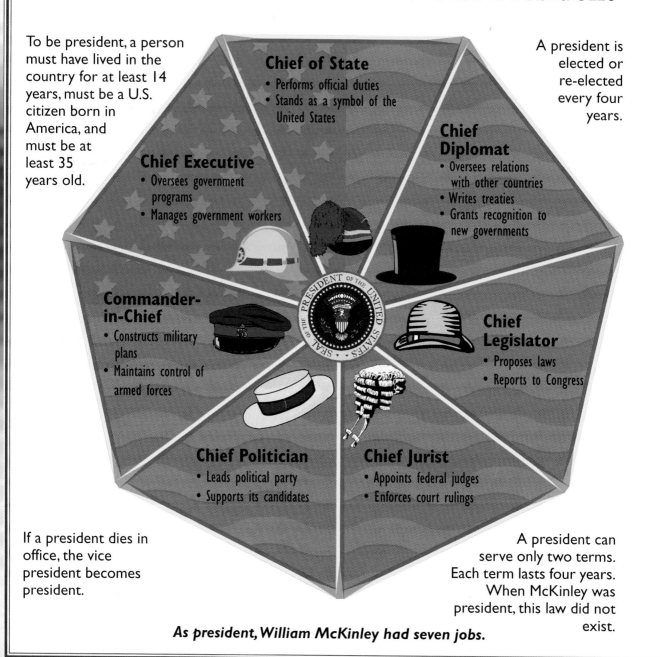

To be president, a person must have lived in the country for at least 14 years, must be a U.S. citizen born in America, and must be at least 35 years old.

A president is elected or re-elected every four years.

Chief of State
- Performs official duties
- Stands as a symbol of the United States

Chief Diplomat
- Oversees relations with other countries
- Writes treaties
- Grants recognition to new governments

Chief Executive
- Oversees government programs
- Manages government workers

Commander-in-Chief
- Constructs military plans
- Maintains control of armed forces

Chief Legislator
- Proposes laws
- Reports to Congress

Chief Politician
- Leads political party
- Supports its candidates

Chief Jurist
- Appoints federal judges
- Enforces court rulings

SEAL OF THE PRESIDENT OF THE UNITED STATES

If a president dies in office, the vice president becomes president.

A president can serve only two terms. Each term lasts four years. When McKinley was president, this law did not exist.

As president, William McKinley had seven jobs.

The Three Branches of the U.S. Government

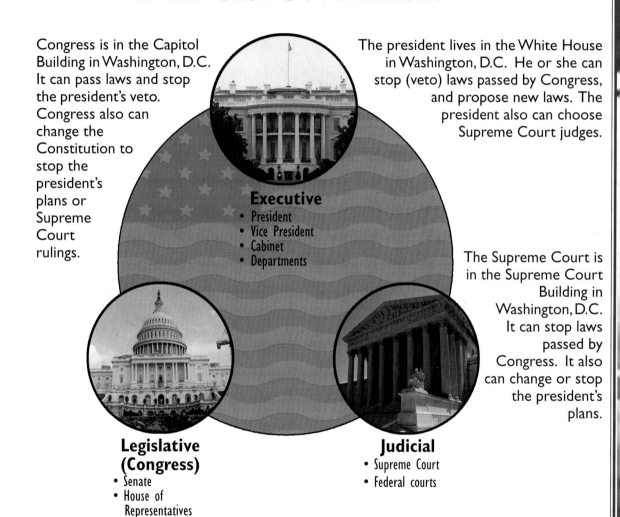

Congress is in the Capitol Building in Washington, D.C. It can pass laws and stop the president's veto. Congress also can change the Constitution to stop the president's plans or Supreme Court rulings.

The president lives in the White House in Washington, D.C. He or she can stop (veto) laws passed by Congress, and propose new laws. The president also can choose Supreme Court judges.

Executive
- President
- Vice President
- Cabinet
- Departments

The Supreme Court is in the Supreme Court Building in Washington, D.C. It can stop laws passed by Congress. It also can change or stop the president's plans.

Legislative (Congress)
- Senate
- House of Representatives

Judicial
- Supreme Court
- Federal courts

The U.S. Constitution formed three government branches. Each branch has power over the others. So, no single group or person can control the country. The Constitution calls this "separation of powers."

A Tragic Ending

*P*resident McKinley's vice president, Garret Hobart, died in office in 1899. The **Republicans** chose New York governor Theodore Roosevelt to succeed him.

In the election of 1900, McKinley and Roosevelt won easily. They got almost 900,000 more popular votes than **Democratic** nominee William Jennings Bryan.

On September 6, 1901, President McKinley was at the Pan-American Exposition in Buffalo, New York. Hundreds of people lined up to shake his hand. One of the guests, Leon Czolgosz, was an anarchist. He believed all government was evil and should be eliminated.

Czolgosz had a gun under a bandage on his hand. When President McKinley reached to shake Czolgosz's hand, he fired the gun twice. He shot the president in the stomach.

President McKinley died eight days later, on September 14, 1901. His last words were: "Good-bye—Good-bye, all. It is God's way. His will, not ours be done." President McKinley was buried in Canton, Ohio.

An illustration of President McKinley's assassination

Fun Facts

- William McKinley had a pet parrot in the White House that could whistle "Yankee Doodle."

- William McKinley was the last **Civil War** veteran to be president of the United States.

- McKinley loved cigars, but he would never be photographed with one because he didn't want to set a bad example for the children of America. He knew they were a very bad habit.

William McKinley

Glossary

blast furnace - an extremely hot furnace used to melt metals.

civil service - the part of the government that runs matters not covered by the military, the courts, or laws.

Civil War - a war between the Union and the Confederate States of America from 1861 to 1865.

Democrat - a political party. When McKinley was president, they supported farmers and landowners.

exclusive - not divided or shared with others.

foreign - from outside the United States.

House of Representatives - a group of people elected by citizens to represent them. They meet in Washington, D.C., and make laws for the nation.

immigration - when people move from one country to another.

lieutenant - an army rank above sergeant and below captain.

major - an army rank above captain and below colonel.

private - the lowest army rank.

prosecutor - a lawyer who argues to convict the person on trial.

Republican - a political party. When McKinley was president, they supported business and strong government.

smelt - to work with metal by heating, melting, and beating it into shapes.

Internet Sites

The Presidents of the United States of America
http://www.whitehouse.gov/WH/glimpse/presidents/html/presidents.html
This site is from the White House. With an introduction from President Bill Clinton and biographies that include each president's inaugural address, this site is excellent. Get information on White House history, art in the White House, first ladies, first families, and much more.

POTUS—Presidents of the United States
http://www.ipl.org/ref/POTUS/
In this resource you will find background information, election results, cabinet members, presidency highlights, and some odd facts on each of the presidents. Links to biographies, historical documents, audio and video files, and other presidential sites are also included to enrich this site.

These sites are subject to change. Go to your favorite search engine and type in United States presidents for more sites.

Pass It On

History enthusiasts: educate readers around the country by passing on information you've learned about presidents or other important people who've changed history. Share your little-known facts and interesting stories. We want to hear from you!

To get posted on the ABDO Publishing Company Web site, email us at:
history@abdopub.com
Visit the ABDO Publishing Company Web site at www.abdopub.com

Index

jB
MCKINLEY   Joseph, Paul.

             William McKinley.

$21.35

DATE			